The Life and Work of...

Mary Cassatt

Ernestine Giesecke

First published in Great Britain by
Heinemann Library,
Halley Court, Jordan Hill, Oxford OX2 8EJ
a division of Reed Educational and Professional Publishing Ltd
Heinemann is a registered trademark of Reed Educational & Professional Publishing Ltd

OXFORD MELBOURNE AUCKLAND
JOHANNESBURG BLANTYRE GABORONE
IBADAN PORTSMOUTH (NH) USA CHICAGO

Printed in Hong Kong/China

03 02 01 00 99
10 9 8 7 6 5 4 3 2 1

ISBN 0 431 09192 7

British Library Cataloguing in Publication Data
Giesecke, Ernestine, 1945-
Life and work of Mary Cassatt
1. Cassatt, Mary, 1844-1926 - Juvenile literature
2. Women painters - United States - Biography - Juvenile literature
3. Painters - United States - Biography - Juvenile literature
4. Painting, American - Juvenile literature
5. Painting, Modern - 19th century - United States - Juvenile literature
I.Title
759.1'3

Acknowledgments
The Publisher would like to thank the following for permission to reproduce photographs:

The Pennsylvania Academy of Fine Arts, Philadelphia, pp. 4, 8; The Denver Art Museum, Anonymous Bequest, p. 5; Drawing of Cassatt Family, Peter Baumgartner, 1854, Anonymous Owner, p. 6; Fine Arts Museums of San Francisco, Museum purchase, William H. Nobel Bequest Fund, 1979.35, p. 7; Founders Society Purchase, Robert H. Tannahill Foundation Fund, The Detroit Institute of Arts, p. 9; Corbis/Bettmann, p. 10; The Roland P. Murdock Collection, Wichita Art Museum, Wichita, Kansas, p.11; Bibliotheque Nationale, Department des Estampes, p. 12; Philadelphia Museum of Art, W.P. Wilstach Collection, p. 13; Erich Lessing/Art Resource, p. 14; Sterling and Francine Clark Art Institute, p. 15; The Bridgeman Art Library International, Ltd., pp. 16, 23; Collection of Mr. and Mrs. Paul Mellon, ©1999 Board of Trustees, National Gallery of Art, Washington, 1878, p.17; National Portrait Gallery, Smithsonian Institution. Gift of the Morris and Gwendolyn Cafritz Foundation and the Regents' Major Acquisitions fund, Smithsonian Institution, p. 18; The Metropolitan Museum of Art, Bequest of Edith H. Proskauer, 1975, p. 19; Anonymous Gift in Honor of Eugenia Cassatt Madeira courtesy, Museum of Fine Arts, Boston, p. 20; M. Theresa B. Hopkins Fund courtesy, Museum of Fine Arts, Boston, p. 21; Photograph ©Bibliotheque Nationale de France, Paris, p. 22; Anonymous Owner, p. 24; Los Angeles County Museum of Art, gift of Mrs. Fred Hathaway Bixby Bequest, p. 25; Lee B. Ewing/F.A. Sweet Papers, Archives of American Art, Smithsonian Institution, p. 26; photograph courtesy of Terra Museum of American Art, Chicago, p. 27.

Cover photo: *Five O'Clock Tea*, Mary Cassatt/M. Theresa B. Hopkins Fund courtesy, Museum of Fine Arts, Boston

Every effort has been made to contact copyright holders of any material reproduced in this book. Any omissions will be rectified in subsequent printings if notice is given to the publisher.

For more information about Heinemann Library books, or to order, please telephone +44(0) 1865 888066, or send a fax to +44(0)1865 314091. You can visit our website at www.heinemann.co.uk

Some words in this book are in bold, **like this.** You can find out what they mean by looking in the Glossary.

Contents

Who was Mary Cassatt?

Mary Cassatt was an American artist. She was a successful woman painter at a time when most painters were men.

Most of Mary's art shows **scenes** from everyday life. Some of her most well-known paintings are of mothers and children.

Early years

Mary was born on 22 May 1844 in Pittsburgh, America. When Mary was seven years old she moved to Paris in France with her family. Two years later they moved to Germany. She was ten years old when this picture was drawn.

At school, Mary **studied** many subjects. She liked drawing and music. She drew whatever was around her. She liked to draw pictures of her family. Mary painted this **portrait** of her mother, Katherine Cassatt, in 1889.

Art student in Philadelphia

In 1855, Mary and her family moved back to America. When Mary was 17 years old she went to the Pennsylvania Academy of Fine Arts. Mary is the girl on the right.

Mary learned to draw from life and by **studying** other works of art. She liked to ride horses with her older brother, Alexander. This is a **portrait** Mary painted of him when she was 36 years old.

Paris

In 1866 Mary went to Paris. She wanted to **study** art. Like other art students, she studied works of art by great artists. She copied their paintings in a museum called the Louvre.

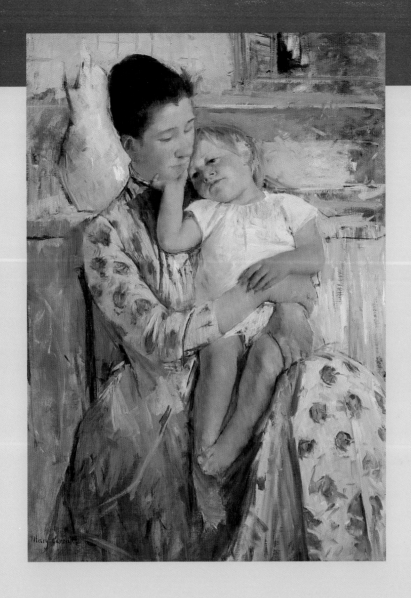

Mary studied **Madonna and Child** paintings. This helped her to paint her own pictures of mothers caring for their small children.

The Salon

In 1868, when Mary was 24 years old, her work was chosen to be shown in the **Salon** in Paris. The Salon was a place where artists who made excellent paintings showed their work.

This painting is called 'On the Balcony during Carnival'. It is like many of the paintings Mary made when she first moved to Paris. It is the kind of painting the Salon judges liked.

Professional artist

Mary **exhibited** in the **Salon** for a few more years. She grew tired of having to paint what would please the judges at the Salon.

Mary did not want to paint **models** anymore.
She did not want to use dark colours. She
wanted to paint things as she saw them.

Changing her ways

In 1877, Mary met an artist called Edgar Degas. Edgar introduced Mary to other painters. These painters were known as the **Impressionists**. The Impressionists painted **scenes** of everyday life.

The Impressionists painted with **splotches** of colour. Mary liked the colours they used and the way they used them. She made this painting in 1878 soon after she met Edgar.

Joining the Impressionists

Mary and Edgar became good friends. They visited each other's **studios.** They talked about their work and gave each other ideas. Edgar Degas painted this **portrait** of Mary.

Mary liked the **Impressionists'** ideas. She used
their ideas in her own paintings. She began to
use lighter colours and looser brushstrokes.
She did this **self-portrait** in 1878.

Painting real life

Most **Impressionists** painted outdoor **scenes**. Mary used the Impressionist ideas but she painted indoor scenes. The paintings tell us about Mary's life.

Most of Mary's paintings are **portraits** of her family, friends and neighbours. Many things in Mary's paintings belonged to her. Look at the silver tea set on page 20. You can see it in the painting on this page.

Painting women

Mary lived in a lively part of Paris near this café.
Painters, musicians, and writers met at cafés to
talk about their ideas. Mary and the women she
knew read newspapers. They wanted to keep up
with the news.

Mary sometimes painted women reading the newspaper. This was something new in painting. At that time, most artists painted **models** who **posed** just for the painting.

Mothers and children

Mary never married or had any children. Mary's brother, Alexander, and his family stayed with her when they visited Europe. Mary loved her nieces and nephews. She often painted pictures of them.

Mary spent hours on each drawing and painting. Yet much of her work shows **scenes** that would be over very quickly. This is a painting of a mother washing her sleepy child.

French countryside

Mary bought a house near Paris. She spent most of her time there. Her **studio** was on the first floor of her home. She could look out onto her pond and gardens.

This picture of ducks was **inspired** by the pond behind Mary's home. This picture is a print. A print allows an artist to make many copies of the same picture. Mary worked hard and became very good at making prints.

A lasting impression

During the last years of Mary's life, her eyesight failed. She could not paint. Mary Cassatt died on 14 June 1926. She was 82 years old.

Mary Cassatt is remembered for her tender pictures of mothers and children.

Timeline

1844	Mary Cassatt born on 22 May in America.
1853	The artist Vincent van Gogh is born in Holland.
1861	Mary begins her studies at Pennsylvania Academy of Fine Arts.
1861–65	U. S. Civil War.
1865–70	Mary travels in Europe.
1868	Mary's work first **exhibited** at the Salon.
1879	Mary exhibits with the **Impressionists**. The artist Paul Klee is born.
1890	The artist Vincent van Gogh dies.
1893	Mary's first individual exhibition.
1900	World's Fair in Paris, France.
1914–18	The First World War. Mary moves to Italy to avoid the war.
1920	Women in the U.S. win the right to vote.
1926	Mary Cassatt dies on 14 June.

Glossary

exhibit to show art in public

Impressionists group of artists who painted outside to make colourful pictures

inspire to influence or guide

Madonna and Child work of art that shows Mary and baby Jesus

model person an artist paints or draws

portrait painting, drawing, or photograph of a person

pose to sit or stand still for an artist

Salon place in Paris where artists were invited to show their artwork

scene place where something happens

self-portrait picture of the artist

splotch large spot

studio place where an artist works

study to learn

More books to read
First Impressions: Mary Cassatt, Susan E Meyer, Harry N Abrams

What makes a Cassatt a Cassatt?, Richard Muhlberger, Cherrytree Books

Looking at Paintings: Children, Peggy Roalf, Belitha Press

More paintings to see
The sisters, Mary Cassatt, Glasgow Art Gallery, Glasgow

Young woman sewing in the garden, Mary Cassatt, Musee d'Orsay, Paris

Mother and child against a green background, Mary Cassatt, Musee d'Orsay, Paris

Index